From Possibility
to Success

Achieving Positive Student Outcomes in Inclusive Classrooms

Patrick Schwarz

Foreword by Harvey "Smokey" Daniels

HEINEMANN
Portsmouth, NH

Heinemann
361 Hanover Street
Portsmouth, NH 03801–3912
www.heinemann.com

Offices and agents throughout the world

Library of Congress Cataloging-in-Publication Data
Schwarz, Patrick.
    From possibility to success : achieving positive student outcomes in inclusive classrooms / Patrick Schwarz ; foreword by Harvey "Smokey" Daniels.
        p. cm.
    Includes bibliographical references.
    ISBN-13: 978-0-325-04668-6
    ISBN-10: 0-325-04668-9
    1. Inclusive education—United States.   2. Learning disabled children—Education—United States.   I. Title.
LC1201.S383 2013
371.9'0460973—dc23   2012045063

Editor: Holly Kim Price
Production: Victoria Merecki
Interior design: Monica Ann Crigler
Composition: Gina Poirier Graphic Design
Cover design: Lisa A. Fowler
Front cover photo: David Stirling
Back cover photo: Natacha Horn, www.natachahorn.com
Manufacturing: Steve Bernier

Printed in the United States of America on acid-free paper
17   16   15   14   13   EBM   1   2   3   4   5

For all of the kids and teachers
(licensed and new teachers) who appear in the book.
You awe me by making common miracles happen every day.
You are the inspirations for this book.

Contents

To download the forms featured throughout this book, please visit www.heinemann.com/products/E04668.aspx.

Foreword

These are challenging times for teachers. Our classrooms are becoming increasingly "multidiverse," welcoming students who have learning, cognitive, or physical disabilities; have ADD/HD; need English language support; face emotional or behavioral challenges; lack interest or engagement; have autism or Asperger syndrome; or are gifted and talented. We know it is best for all these kids, and for the wider community, that everyone be educated in the regular classroom to the greatest extent possible. But how?

In this era of national standards and testing, the pressure on teachers to meet a wide range of needs grows ever greater, but practical supports seem hard to find. The conversation too often focuses on students as "data" and teaching methods as "delivery systems," with teachers judged by their "fidelity" to mandated programs. If you are a teacher sincerely eager to support a wide range of learners in your classroom but need some concrete and principled guidance, this book is for you.

As with all of Patrick's work, stories of real kids are at its heart. So get ready to meet Max, Sophie, Trevor, Josh, Dan, Brian, Marcel, Bridget, Gabriel, Christopher, Jonah, Brooklyn, Jack, Harley, Angelica, Bill, Anita, Marianne, Joelle, Matthew, and many more learners who deserve the thoughtful and caring support of their teachers. And watch how those teachers listen, think, act, adjust, accommodate, and provide challenge in their classrooms.

The practicality and explicitness of this book are hard to beat. Patrick gives you detailed lesson designs, forms, lists, and handouts—all the tools you need to plan for *everyone* in your classroom. He uses the flexible model of universal design to show how to set goals for all, for some, and for a few students—and offers formative assessments that reveal when kids have achieved these goals.

Patrick is not afraid to say that school should be pleasant and enjoyable. There are really only two ways that schools can get kids engaged in the curriculum: coercion or curiosity. Patrick's book is a clarion call for curiosity. If all kids can dream, follow their passion, make choices, take responsibility, and be allowed to work hard, most of the problems of dealing with diversity disappear. As coauthor of a book about best practice K–12, now in its fourth edition, I feel that Patrick has written the best-practice companion text for differentiating instruction in the inclusive classroom.

I know you'll devour every practical, passionate, and powerful page of this book. And I also wish you the opportunity to experience Patrick "live." The passion you can sense between the lines here explodes in a workshop setting, where Patrick will have you laughing, crying, dancing, working with strangers, and making an unforced recommitment to look more closely and think more deeply about all the kids in your classroom. Patrick Schwarz is a gift to our profession and to all the kids in our schools. Happy reading and teaching!

Harvey "Smokey" Daniels

Acknowledgments

Thank you to the many students, teachers, and families who inspired me in this book through your stories, beliefs, convictions, and actions, turning possibility into success.

I am massively grateful to my loved ones for their major support with this book. Thanks Bill, for being an amazing editor before the other editors got to look at it! Your ideas, positive feedback, honesty, integrity, and insightfulness immensely strengthened this book and provided a clarity that was moving to me. Thank you to Katie and Haley for continuing to inspire, and Dan and Becca for providing new inspiration by teaching me important concepts of possibility and success through your stories. Vicky, Mom, Bob, Tim, and Sarah, you continue to cheer me on and it feels very good. I genuinely appreciate all of the kindness and support from my new family, Ed, Laurie, Gary, Gil, Marliss, Stacy, David, Caryn, Howard, Sheila, Andrea, Chris, Jack, Stephen, Ann, Juliana, Ellis, Janet, and Melinda.

I have amazing colleagues that are major professional forces in this field. Paula Kluth, you constantly move me with your brilliant viewpoints and the energy you use to relay them. I am thankful you are in the field every day because you make the world a better place. I look forward to collaborating with you on future works! Alice Udvari-Solner, your wisdom and conviction with supporting people in a landmark way put me through a belief boot camp when I first started practicing in the field. You are a superb paradigm pioneer, yet so kind, humble, spiritual, and never comfortable with anything, since you are always taking the next step—wow! Smokey Daniels, you have always been here for me and wrote my favorite 2009 educational book on inquiry circles with Stephanie Harvey. Your ability to positively change schools makes learning work for all! The foreword you wrote for this book brought tears to my eyes and thanks for all you have taught me. Huge appreciation goes to Lou Brown, Anne Donnellan, Kurt Schneider, Jacque Thousand, Richard Villa, Norman Kunc, and Emma Van der Klift for changing lives, including mine, through your work!

My friends are a never-ending support through listening, knowing when to push me off the soapbox and providing all around fun. Thank you Bucky, Sandy, Tracy, Natacha, Kassira, Todd, and Victoria for being you.

Tanita, you are a very special artistic friend who astutely understands the writing and performing process, which helps me to be a better writer, presenter, and facilitator. I am always moved by the quality you expect of yourself and therefore you are a significant model. Your kindness, communication, support, and beliefs mean the world to me.

Early on before the book was written and my annotated table of contents was being developed, Anita Gildea from Heinemann believed in my ideas immediately. She pitched the book to a team of editors and made the next steps a reality. Thank you Anita for getting it.

Huge special recognition goes out to Holly Kim Price, who took one look at my annotated table of contents and shared to all, "I want to be the editor of this book." As the editor, you have been astute in your understanding of my viewpoints and a professional soulmate in your beliefs and learner-centeredness. Your support, ideas, and quality expectations are admirable. You are a huge part of making this book a reality.

In addition, thank you also to Alan Huisman for his great editorial work and Victoria Merecki for her strong production work. To Lisa Fowler who beautifully designed the cover and made my idea come alive, to David Stirling for his brilliant photography and to Monica Ann Crigler for the great interior design. I am so grateful to my amazing team from Heinemann.

Finally, thank you to all the students, families, school systems, professional organizations, and universities that I have the honor to work with through my presentations, workshops, and consultations. It is clearly important to me to get this message out to people. I am so honored you have heard it and want more people to hear it.

Introduction

General education and special education are in a constant state of evolution and change. School districts can no longer refer all students with nonstandard learning needs for special education services, and that's as it should be. While our learning population becomes more diverse in ability and need for support, state boards and departments of education are clearly communicating that we need to keep learners who need special education services to 10 percent or 12 percent of the school population (Fisher, Frey, and Rothenberg 2010).

This is a difficult (and sometimes unattainable) goal in schools and districts with the traditional approach to diverse learners: *let special education take care of them.* In addition, scientific methods for determining who does and does not receive special education services can knock the wind out of many teachers' sails, obstructing educational innovation (Zemelman, Daniels, and Hyde 2012).

In the years since *From Disability to Possibility: The Power of Inclusive Classrooms* was published, teaching has become more a science, less an art:

- There is a greater focus on standards-based education, requiring additions and revisions in federal, state, and professional group methods and curriculums.
- Expectations regarding response to intervention (RtI) continue to increase.
- Tests scores are scrutinized ever more closely.
- Comparisons of school district test scores create a culture of competition.
- Educators opt to teach to the test.
- More and more teachers depend on ability groupings.

In addition, learning diversity continues to increase throughout our country and world. One in every sixty-one children now has some degree of autism (Fein 2011). Many students lack interest and engagement. Many have been up most of the night playing video and computer games, fast-paced activities derived from someone else's creativity.

What does the reality that 97 percent of teenage males and 94 percent of teenage females report gaming as a pastime (McCall 2011) and parents are best able to contact their teenage sons or daughters by texting them say about teaching and assessment?

I am not the king of gloom and doom. In *From Disability to Possibility*, I hypothesized that there is a way out, a better manner to proceed. I still believe that. Successful teachers who embrace the art of their profession can make learning work for all. The key questions are:

- How do we make all the changes taking place in education work for rather than against what we know is good for learners?

- How do we keep the art of teaching intact while meeting its requirements as a science?

- How do we get teachers and leaders to embrace rather than begrudge meeting the needs of all learners?

- How do we learn from the ways students experience and use technology in their daily lives?

- How do we focus on best and promising practices and successful learning for all students during their entire school career, learning that will enhance their quality of life?

Successful teachers who embrace the art of their profession can make learning work for all.

This book, *From Possibility to Success: Achieving Positive Student Outcomes in Inclusive Classrooms*, proposes educational resuscitation: practices, processes, and tools that address the scientific requirements of teaching diverse learners while bringing back the art of teaching all learners. Each chapter introduces a new tool for success, provides the rationale for using it, and shares compelling stories of how it has helped real students in real classrooms. The tools are:

1. Universal Design for Learning/Differentiated Instruction/Individual Accommodation Lesson Plan Template (Chapter 1).

2. Interests/Favorites Inventory (Chapter 2).

3. Student Dream Inventory (Chapter 3).

4. Teacher/Family/Counselor Talking Points for Identifying Student Dreams (Chapter 4).

5. Promoting Student Leadership, Self-Advocacy, Decision Making, and Self-Determination (Chapter 5).

6. Effective Group-Work Options to Achieve a Collaborative and Cooperative Classroom Community (Chapter 6).

7. Supporting Student Needs Within the Classroom Community (Chapter 7).

8. Developing Student Presence Map in the School and Wider Communities (Chapter 8).

9. Three-Day Unit on Understanding and Embracing Learner Diversity (Chapter 9).

10. Student Priorities/Action Plan at a Glance (Chapter 10).

This book is intended to give hope, direction, and inspiration. The goal is learner success and achievement in the classroom and beyond. If you are a general educator, a special educator, a provider of related services, a para-educator, or an administrator who has lost the art of and passion for what you are doing and want to bring it back, read on. If you are a parent, share it with a teacher for ideas and support to address the greater learning diversity in her or his classroom.

This book is intended to give hope, direction, and inspiration. The goal is learner success and achievement in the classroom and beyond.

Chapter **One**

Build the Foundation

Meet All Students' Needs Through Universal Design for Learning, Differentiated Instruction, and Individual Accommodations

The students in today's classrooms are multidiverse—in ways of learning, cultural backgrounds, family structures, ways of life. The key to unlocking their potential is to meet the educational needs of a spectrum of learners that includes those who are gifted and talented; have learning, cognitive, or physical disabilities; have ADD/HD; need English language support; face emotional or behavioral challenges; lack interest or engagement; have autism or Asperger syndrome. Including all students in the same general education classroom allows them to belong everywhere and with everyone else in the school, which in turn allows them to belong everywhere and with everyone else in the community (Schwarz 2006). Providing segregated places and spaces for students with disabilities promulgates continued segregation in the community after graduation and sends the message that individuals with disabilities are visitors in rather than members of society.

> *Including all students in the same general education classroom allows them to belong everywhere and with everyone else in the school, which in turn allows them to belong everywhere and with everyone else in the community.*

To achieve success, the curriculum must work for all learners. Once it does, teachers can focus on building lifelong skills for the future by embracing learner interests and passions; capturing and working toward learners' dreams; and promoting leadership, self-advocacy, self-determination, and membership in the school and the community. This chapter explains how to plan lessons and units that incorporate universal learning design, differentiated instruction, and individual accommodation, the building blocks of successful learning.

UNIVERSAL LEARNING DESIGN: OPEN THE DOORS WIDE

Universal learning design (CAST Universal Design for Learning 2012) considers all students individuals and offers multiple, multifaceted ways of making learning work for everyone. I think of universal learning design as *access for all*. It parallels other ways we accommodate diversity—curb cuts or ramps, for example. When I broke my foot kick-boxing several years ago and had to use crutches for six weeks, I was very thankful for curb cuts when I was crossing streets. They enabled me to make my way more smoothly and more quickly.

Here's another example. After I had taught the first class in one of my university courses, Kelly came to me and told me she was deaf. I replied, "How can I help you?" She suggested several ways:

- Preferential seating. She wanted to be able to see my face well because she was an adept lip-reader. This would help her "hear" all the information I provided orally.

- There were still going to be times when she wouldn't be able to see my face or lips. If a student she knew were seated next to her, he could tell her what she missed.

- Films or video clips should be closed-captioned or accompanied by a study guide.

In order to give Kelly the support she needed, I got to every class early and reserved seats for her and her friend at the front of the classroom. I also used closed-captioned films or provided study guides. Kelly, a role model for self-advocacy and self-determination, did well in the class and is now a successful teacher.

Universal learning design has three major components: multiple means of representation, multiple means of engagement, and multiple means of expression.

> **I** *think of universal learning design as* **access** *for all.*

Multiple Means of Representation: Make Content Work

Means of representation are how content is presented to students. Examples that help meet the needs of all learners include offering audio and visual options at all times, providing guided notes and graphic organizers during a lecture or review, and offering books at different reading levels that provide different levels of understanding.

Ms. White: Relate to Everyone

Recently, I observed Ms. White, a third-grade teacher, provide various means of representation to her students. First she introduced a nonfiction trade book, *Teammates* (Golenbock and Bacon 1992), about the history of the famous baseball player Jackie Robinson, and asked students to look at photographs in the book and predict what might happen in the story. Students displayed their predictions on an electronic whiteboard and discussed each one. Next, she asked students to locate words in the book they did not understand, display them, and discuss their meaning. The student who had contributed the word then looked it up and added the definition to the whiteboard. After these inquiry steps, Ms. White had students listen to the first chapter on an audio version of the book as they followed along in their copy. Afterward, she let them choose whether they wanted to finish reading the book alone, with a group, or continue with the audio version (which anticipates multiple means of engagement).

Multiple Means of Engagement:
Pave Many Learning Pathways

Means of engagement are the pathways through which students learn and understand—the ways we make learning interesting. They are particularly important in light of the lack of interest and engagement sometimes shown by today's learners. Examples include embracing student interests and providing lessons based on inquiry and investigation that promote active mental and physical engagement and lead to real understanding. Allowing students to choose how they will complete their assignments, applications, and responsibilities encourages them to participate actively and effectively. Examples include working independently, with a partner, or in small groups; working at a desk, at a table, or on the floor; and using technology inside or outside the classroom (see the Max example below). Some students need to write to understand, others need to talk through ideas, and still others may need to represent what they are learning physically or graphically.

> *Allowing students to choose how they will complete their assignments, applications, and responsibilities encourages them to participate actively and effectively.*

Max: Provide Options for All

Max, a learner with ADHD, was a member of a general education fourth-grade class. His individual education plan (IEP) stated that he needed a quiet place in which to work, and he typically did so in the library. One day Max did not want to leave the classroom; he struggled with his special educator, Mrs. C., who insisted he come with her. His general education teacher, Ms. Abzul, was bothered by the incident for the rest of the day. The next day she changed the options for completing work. Students could:

- Work alone at their desk.
- Work with a peer at a desk, speaking just above a whisper.
- Work alone on the floor.
- Work with a peer on the floor, speaking just above a whisper.
- Go to the library with Mrs. C., who usually worked there alone with Max.

The flexibility of these choices honored the idea that the students were all individuals and had preferences in the way they wanted to complete their work. The message the day before had been that Max did not belong in the classroom when everyone else was working—that he was a visitor. When the library was a choice for all, Max became a full-fledged member of the class, not just a sometime visitor.

One day after these options had been in place for a while, Max again decided he would rather do his work in the classroom than in the library. Mrs. Abzul said he could stay in the classroom with her while Mrs. C. went to the library with those who wanted to go there, thereby giving Max the same choices everyone else had, empowering him, and helping him advocate for himself. Max did just fine working in the classroom; he had grown over time and made progress with his educational goals, a cause for celebration! No one stays the same forever, and we have to honor that notion for all students. Isn't progress what we hope for and dream as the outcome of learning?

George Theoharis and Julie Causton-Theoharis (2010) have studied the practice of pulling out students to receive special education services. They found that the more significant the disability, the more often the student was pulled out, for longer periods—which is the exact opposite of what students with significant challenges need. Students with more significant disabilities need an ongoing, consistent schedule and a learning environment in which they are led from one concept to the next. Yet in many school districts students with significant challenges have the most fragmented schedules of anyone in the school. The purpose of related services in schools is to *support the educational program*; they are not a separate program unrelated to the daily life of the general education classroom. The Theoharis/Causton-Theoharis study supports educating all students in the least restrictive environment—the general education classroom. Zemelman, Daniels, and Hyde (2012) also promote pulling diverse learners out of the general classroom less often.

Offering students choices for how they do their work is important in all grades, preschool through high school, because students in higher education have many options for where and how they study. When I was a student at the University of Wisconsin–Madison, I had several. First, there was the Memorial Library, which was so quiet you could hear a pin drop. There were people whose job was "shushing." If somebody talked or made too much noise, they would look the individual straight in the eye and say, "Shhhh!" I clearly could not work in that environment! Next, there was the Helen C. White Library. I liked this library because it had tables at which you could converse quietly with others. There was also a writing laboratory on the second floor. Every time I wrote a paper, I got to the point where I couldn't look at it anymore; it really helped to have a lab staff member offer editorial commentary and advice. The third option was the Memorial Student Union. The first floor had a room called the Rathskeller, where students were always talking, laughing, and having drinks at round wooden tables. Music was always playing, and it was often loud. I found it a bit too loud and wild for studying, but it was a great place to go when I wasn't. Above the Rathskeller was a beautiful, well-lit room with lots of windows and a wonderful view of Lake Mendota. It had comfortable lounge-type furniture, and classical music played all the time. This was my favorite place to work!

In what setting or settings do you like to work? Must it be completely quiet? Must you be alone? Or do you like the murmur of soft voices? Do you need comfortable furniture? Do you like to sit or lie on the floor? What about music? What kind and how loud? Offering students a range of choices for where and how they do their work lets them get it done more quickly with less stress and lets them discover their future preferences as adults. Of course, we don't get to choose everything in life, so yes, we sometimes assign specific conditions and means for how students work. When we give students choices about how they do their work, are we potentially promoting better work? If you think the answer is even remotely yes, offer choices.

> *The purpose of related services in schools is to* support the educational program; they are not *a separate program unrelated to the daily life of the general education classroom.*

Multiple Means of Expression: Express Yourself

Means of expression are how students express and demonstrate what they have learned. Authentic expression takes many paths. Traditional paper-and-pencil tests are very limiting for many students; others do fine on them. Other assessment options include projects, tiered assignments, multimedia demonstrations, models, films, portfolios, oral exams, etc.

Sophie: Offer a Choice

Sophie is a friendly and energetic fifth-grader; she also has ADHD as an attribute. Her teacher, Ms. Kweller, taught Sophie's class a unit on ecology and "going green." To demonstrate their understanding of the unit's concepts, students had three options: (1) they could write a paper discussing at least three ways their family could go green at home (this option appealed to learners with verbal-linguistic intelligence); (2) they could design a poster depicting at least three ways their family could go green at home (this option appealed to learners with visual-spatial intelligence); or (3) they could contact a local business and interview a member of management about at least three ways the company has made their work environment green (this option appealed to learners with interpersonal intelligence). Sophie chose to create the poster. She loved to illustrate and used many colored markers. Her finished poster clearly showed her passion and talent for illustration and her understanding of green ecology. At the end of the year, Sophie identified the ecology unit as her favorite; being able to complete a meaningful project played an important role in her feelings.

> **W**hen we give students choices about how they do their work, are we potentially promoting better work? If you think the answer is even remotely yes, offer choices.

DIFFERENTIATED INSTRUCTION: CONSIDER EVERYONE

Differentiated instruction is mandatory in today's classrooms. General educators must plan for all learners, including those with individualized education plans. The notion of *your students* and *my students* must give way to *our students*. Differentiation is very much a general education issue, even though many of the schools I encounter in my work view it as related to special education only. Because of the diverse learning styles and needs of students in all classrooms these days, any lesson or unit must include differentiation that will meet most student needs, including those with individualized education plans. Special educators, bilingual teachers, and other service professionals, in conjunction with the classroom teacher, can then create accommodations to meet the needs of students who need additional support. Identifying learning targets that *all* students in the classroom need to achieve, that *most* students need to achieve, and that *some* students need to achieve will make every lesson meaningful for every student and promote and maximize participation. The same applies to assessment targets. Planning assessment targets that *all* students need to demonstrate (and the options for doing so), that *most* students need to demonstrate (and the options for doing so), and that *some* students need to demonstrate (and the options for doing so) ensures that all lessons are meaningful and can be undertaken via a variety of pathways.

INDIVIDUAL ACCOMMODATION: TAKE IT FURTHER FOR SOME

Even jumping from the springboard of a differentiated lesson, some students still need individual accommodations in the form of materials, technology, and procedures. Accommodations zero in on specific learning needs. Specialists often design and implement individual accommodations in collaboration with the general educator. One example is an individual schedule in a student's notebook or iPad for every part of the school day, including any changes from the routine, in order to prevent potentially adverse reactions and promote learning and using lifelong skills.

Mason: Bring On Accommodations

Mason was a curious young kindergartner with a big smile. He walked around the classroom and playground, paying attention to everything and periodically hitting other students. He smiled while hitting the other students, but since his smile was constant it didn't necessarily mean he enjoyed hitting them. He had not yet been identified as requiring special education services, but his general education placement was at risk. Mason's family wanted him to remain in his general education classroom; the school was considering segregation. Mason's family retained an attorney, as did the school. I was asked to make an evaluation.

Mason's hitting seemed random, his physical well-being a bit off-kilter. I thought he would benefit from sensory experiences that helped him feel more together and able to cope with the world. I requested that a colleague of mine, Tracy Lyndon, a private occupational therapist with expertise in sensory integration in all settings, including schools, evaluate Mason.

Tracy agreed that Mason needed sensory integration support. She suggested he be permitted to use a little scooter to get around and use a swing on the playground. In addition, Tracy introduced classroom routines that incorporated sensory support options for everyone so that Mason's differences would seem less unusual. For example, students could sit on cushions, therapy balls, or T-squares and manipulate stress balls and widgets. They were also introduced to scents like peppermint and orange and allowed to eat a piece of hard candy or chew gum. (A number of school districts now provide cinnamon gum for students to chew while taking standardized tests.) Other examples include being able to choose writing instruments of different sizes and grips and to change position in the classroom.

Mason quickly seemed more physically together, more focused and engaged throughout the school day. He stopped hitting other students in the classroom and on the playground. Many other students in the classroom became more focused and engaged as well. Goodbye lawyers!

MAKE IT OPERATIONAL

The template below was initially developed by Dr. Valerie Owen in her work with the Chicago International Charter schools; it was based on the work of Mager (1988); Schumm, Vaughn, and Harris (1998); and Wiggins and McTighe (1998); as well as on concepts formulated by CAST and Carol Tomlinson. The version here was designed by Valerie Owen, Donna Wakefield, Elizabeth Grace, and me. After being introduced to this lesson plan format during our university's teacher education training program, our graduates say they use it to plan all their lessons, and their students are more successful learners.

The more you use the format, the easier it gets. Paying greater attention to universal learning design, differentiated instruction, and individual accommodation ensures that learning targets are met more effectively. I recommend you first use the template that includes explanations. As you become more comfortable with the concepts, you'll no longer need the explanations and can use the streamlined template.

> *Paying greater attention to universal learning design, differentiated instruction, and individual accommodation ensures that learning targets are met more effectively.*

DIRECTIONS FOR USING DIFFERENTIATED INSTRUCTION/UNIVERSAL DESIGN FOR LEARNING LESSON/UNIT PLANNING TEMPLATE

1. **Identify the Lesson Topic**
    An electronic or manual filing system lets you find and replicate lessons when needed.

2. **Identify Related Common Core Learning Standards**
    Acknowledging the *science* of instruction upfront paves the way to being able to practice the art of teaching.

3. **Differentiate Lesson Content (Identify Learning Targets for All, Most, and Some)**
    First ask: "What are the learning targets that *all* students need to know?" These are the *essential* learning targets. Next ask: "What are the learning targets that *most* students need to know?" These are the *expected* learning targets. Then ask: "What are the learning targets that *some* students need to know?" These are the *enrichment* learning targets.

Don't fall into the trap of equating these learning targets with high-, medium-, and low-ability groups. Those simplistic, linear labels do a great injustice to learners, because they don't take into account the strengths, specialties, passions, interests, and fascinations each learner brings to the table. This lesson planning template does *not* enable or promote ability grouping. Rather, it gives teachers a way to meet every student's needs and gives every student an environment in which he or she can learn.

Also consider the relationship between this planning process and response to intervention (RtI): they share similar goals. In RtI, learning interventions provide successful learning support in general education classrooms so that students don't have to be referred for special education services. This lesson plan template delineates and expands learning and assessment targets to ensure the learning needs of all students are met.

> *T*hose simplistic, linear labels do a great injustice to learners, because they don't take into account the strengths, specialties, passions, interests, and fascinations each learner brings to the table.

4. **Differentiate Assessment (Identify Assessment Targets for All, Most, and Some)**

    First ask: "What are the assessment targets that *all* students need to demonstrate and how will they demonstrate them?" These are the *essential* assessment targets. Next ask: "What are the assessment targets that *most* students need to demonstrate and how will they demonstrate them?" These are the *expected* assessment targets. Then ask: "What are the assessment targets that *some* students need to demonstrate and how will they demonstrate them?" These are the *enrichment* assessment targets.

    Once again, ability groups or traditional assessments are not being promoted. Instead, this universal-design approach systematizes multiple assessments during lessons, units, and projects. It is best practice in supporting learning for all.

5. **Provide Feedback, Record Progress or Needs, and Use Assessment Information**

    Ask the following questions:

    ■ How will I provide feedback to students?

    ■ How will I record progress or needs?

    ■ How will I use assessment information to make instructional decisions?

    Involving students in their own assessment and recording progress is a best practice and needs to be planned.

6. **Identify Multiple Means of Representation, Engagement, and Expression**

    Each area of universal learning design has a different focus. Multiple means of *representation*: "How will I present my content so it meets the needs of each student in the classroom?" Multiple means of *engagement*: "How will I provide multiple pathways for students to learn the material presented and make it interesting?" Multiple means of *expression*: "How will I create many pathways for students to demonstrate what they have learned?"

7. **Identify Materials**

   Identify and prepare needed materials. If you are presenting the lesson with another teacher, specify who is responsible for what.

8. **Specify Technology to Support Learning**

   Specify software, apps, programs, and search engines that support and enhance the lesson. Some technology may be used by just a few students (or even just one student).

9. **Determine Lesson Procedures (Anticipatory Set, Teaching Act, Guided Practice, and Closure)**

   Madeline Hunter's approach to lesson planning (see Cooper et al. 2001) works well here. For the anticipatory set, specify how you will motivate students during your introduction and assess or review their prior knowledge. For the teaching act, your guiding question is, "How do I present this lesson so that each student learns?" Guided practice options include working alone, working with others, and working in a variety of locations. Closure summarizes the current lesson and provides continuity between lessons.

10. **Identify Needed Individual Accommodations**

    Identify and plan accommodations necessary for individual students to be able to participate in the lesson. This creates a supportive classroom community in which every student learns and is assessed.

This universal-design approach systematizes multiple assessments during lessons, units, and projects. It is best practice in supporting learning for all.

Differentiated Instruction/Universal Design for Learning | Lesson/Unit Plan Template

Lesson/Unit Topic

Related Common Core Learning Standards

Differentiation of Lesson Content:
Every student is an individual, having strengths and challenges; therefore learning target areas change for each student's subjects depending on their learning profile.

Essential Learning Targets	Expected Learning Targets	Enrichment Learning Targets
What ALL students will learn:	What MOST students will learn:	What SOME students will learn:

Differentiation of Assessment

Essential Assessment Targets	Expected Assessment Targets	Enrichment Assessment Targets
What ALL students will demonstrate:	What MOST students will demonstrate:	What SOME students will demonstrate:

Student Feedback and How Progress Will Be Recorded

How will you provide feedback for your students? How will you record progress or needs? How will you use this information?

(continues)

(continued)

Elements of Universal Design

Multiple Means of Representation

How are you going to present your content so that it meets the needs of all students? Is the information represented in different ways? For example, offering audio and visual options at all times, utilizing guided notes and graphic organizers during a lecture/review, or having several books that represent different reading and understanding levels helps to meet the learning needs of all.

Multiple Means of Engagement

How are you going to provide multiple pathways for students to actually learn the material presented and make it interesting? How will you engage all learners? Embracing student interests in the classroom, inquiry, investigative learning, active/mental/physical engagement is required by students to make real learning happen. Are choices given to students for how they can do their work? Options may include working independently, pair learning, small-group learning, at a desk, table, floor, using technology, inside the classroom, or outside the classroom. How will feedback be given to keep students motivated? Some students will need to write, others will need to talk through ideas before they understand, while others may need to physically or graphically represent what they are learning.

Multiple Means of Expression

How will students demonstrate what they have learned? The creation of many paths is the key. Some students are good test-takers, while others are not. Projects, tiered assignments, oral exams, building a model, making a film, or creating a portfolio are examples of alternatives to traditional paper/pencil tests.

Materials

What materials do you need for this lesson? Make sure you have all of your materials collected and organized so your lesson will flow smoothly. If you are presenting this lesson collaboratively, make sure you know who is responsible for what.

Technology (Computer and/or Assistive) to Support Learning

Lesson/Unit Procedures	Individual Accommodations Needed for Participation
These will be different for each lesson but should generally include the following: • Anticipatory Set (How are you going to motivate your students, assess or review prior knowledge, and introduce your topic?) • Teaching Act (How will you provide access?) • Guided Practice or other applications • Closure	

Owen, Schwarz, Wakefield, and Grace (2012)*

*This lesson plan was originally developed through work by Dr. Valerie Owen with the Chicago International Charter schools and was based on the work of others, including Mager (1987); Schumm, Vaughn, and Harris (1997); and Wiggins and McTighe (1998), as well as concepts of UDL from CAST and concepts of differentiation from Carol Tomlinson. Dr. Patrick Schwarz, Dr. Donna Wakefield, and Dr. Elizabeth Grace all made additions that appear in this template.

Differentiated Instruction/Universal Design for Learning | Lesson/Unit Plan Template

Lesson/Unit Topic

Related Common Core Learning Standards

Differentiation of Lesson Content

Essential Learning Targets	Expected Learning Targets	Enrichment Learning Targets

Differentiation of Assessment

Essential Assessment Targets	Expected Assessment Targets	Enrichment Assessment Targets

Student Feedback and How Progress Will Be Recorded

(continues)

(continued)

Elements of Universal Design
Multiple Means of Representation
Multiple Means of Engagement
Multiple Means of Expression
Materials
Technology (Computer and/or Assistive) to Support Learning

Lesson/Unit Procedures	Individual Accommodations Needed for Participation
• Anticipatory Set: • Teaching Act: • Guided: • Closure:	

Owen, Schwarz, Wakefield, and Grace (2012)*

*This lesson plan was originally developed through work by Dr. Valerie Owen with the Chicago International Charter schools and was based on the work of others, including Mager (1987); Schumm, Vaughn, and Harris (1997); and Wiggins and McTighe (1998), as well as concepts of UDL from CAST and concepts of differentiation from Carol Tomlinson. Dr. Patrick Schwarz, Dr. Donna Wakefield, and Dr. Elizabeth Grace all made additions that appear in this template.

Example

Differentiated Instruction/Universal Design for Learning | Lesson/Unit Plan Template

Lesson/Unit Topic

Sustaining the Earth by Recycling

Related Common Core Learning Standards

Students develop and apply the knowledge, perspective, vision, skills, and habits of mind necessary to make personal and collective decisions and take actions that promote sustainability. (Integrated and Environmental Sustainability Education Learning Standard 3)

Differentiation of Lesson Content

Essential Learning Targets	Expected Learning Targets	Enrichment Learning Targets
Participate in class discussion on recycling benefits to the environment. Locate 3–5 examples of how and why materials such as plastic and paper are recycled. Provide a list of 3–5 recycling benefits. Find examples and evidence where recycling has made a difference.	Identify and list 3–5 recycling examples taking place in the school and the community. Identify and list 3–5 ways how local recycling programs could be improved in the school or community. Draft a persuasive letter that explains the beneficial aspects of recycling and how it can be improved. Include ideas about how members of the community can help make it work. Proofread letter and create a final draft.	Use written lists of recycling information, ideas, and benefits collected for developing a group proposal to convince school and/or community stakeholders to initiate or renew a recycling program. Write press releases for the event and invite television reporters to attend. Write thank-you notes to stakeholders who attended the event and acknowledge their recycling efforts. Attend applicable community meetings to follow up with what happened to proposals.

Differentiation of Assessment

Essential Assessment Targets	Expected Assessment Targets	Enrichment Assessment Targets
Demonstration of a quality discussion about recycling and benefits to community will be assessed according to a discussion rubric by students and teacher. Written examples and lists will be shared with student groups and written feedback will be provided by each group.	Lists will be assessed by ensuring there are 3–5 quality ideas on each. Students will have opportunity to add further ideas to lists. Students will be assessed on how they use letter template and the given feedback to strengthen letters.	Proposals will be evaluated by other groups and each group can complete a final draft. Students will receive a model of a press release and components list. Each group will self-assess using the model to ensure all components are included.

Student Feedback and How Progress Will Be Recorded

Groups will get feedback from teacher, other groups, and the individual members of their group. Progress will be recorded by teacher in assessment book through use of feedback on actual artifacts. Information will be used to target needed areas of teaching and support for next unit.

(continues)

(continued)

Elements of Universal Design

Multiple Means of Representation

Discussion will be modeled by teacher.

Teacher will explain and provide written model for each list on Promethean board.

Teacher will explain how to create a persuasive letter and proposal. A written handout with a model of a persuasive letter and a proposal will be provided. The persuasive letter and proposal will have a graphic organizer for student use.

Multiple Means of Engagement

Students are able to think through ideas individually, talk through ideas with a group, and work with a group to create lists, the letter, and proposal.

Teacher will ensure that all students gain a balance between intrapersonal and interpersonal work with choices throughout their work.

Multiple Means of Expression

Students will make decisions about how lists, letters, and the proposal are laid out and how the content is presented.

Students get choice about fonts, graphics, and any other visual enhancements they wish to use for letters and proposals.

Materials

Discussion rubric, list examples, letter example, proposal example, letter graphic organizer, proposal graphic organizer

Technology (Computer and/or Assistive) to Support Learning

Students will use computers or an iPad to lay out the letter and proposal designs.

Lesson/Unit Procedures	Individual Accommodations Needed for Participation
• Anticipatory Set: Teacher will fire students up about the importance of recycling by showing pictures of environmentally sound places and places that have been environmentally destroyed. This will be prior to the discussion and will assist in making the discussion and other components of the unit engaging. • Teaching Act: Each learning target is the basis of the teaching act. Teacher will start with essential learning targets and move toward expected and enrichment learning targets as students acquire skills. Access is provided by allowing students to move through targets by understanding and challenge needs. • Guided Practice or other applications: The teacher is a model throughout the unit in the areas of discussion, lists, letter, and proposal. Students also receive guidance through visual models of lists, letter, and proposal. Students also receive a graphic organizer for the letter and proposal. Teacher will monitor and support all students working in groups. • Closure: At the end of the unit, teacher will have students report what they will be doing to promote the concept of recycling in their lives and follow up with actions accomplished.	Program letter and proposal graphic organizers into Nikki's iPad. Provide support with Taylor participating with group as needed. Create unit word bank for James.

Owen, Schwarz, Wakefield, and Grace (2012)*

*This lesson plan was originally developed through work by Dr. Valerie Owen with the Chicago International Charter schools and was based on the work of others, including Mager (1987); Schumm, Vaughn, and Harris (1997); and Wiggins and McTighe (1998), as well as concepts of UDL from CAST and concepts of differentiation from Carol Tomlinson. Dr. Patrick Schwarz, Dr. Donna Wakefield, and Dr. Elizabeth Grace all made additions that appear in this template.

Chapter **Two**

Promote Passion

Everyone has passions, interests, and areas of fascination that make life interesting, engaging, and worthwhile. Paula Kluth and I recently wrote two books about this: *Just Give Him the Whale* (for educators and families) and *Pedro's Whale* (for children). While these books focus on learners with autism, the practice of embracing student passions, interests, and areas of fascination applies to all students. Alfie Kohn states that the most important thing teachers do is to develop a relationship with their students (Kohn 2006). Embracing learner interests and passions is an outstanding way to make connections and establish relationships. It also helps students build trust and make academic gains and can prevent disruptive behavior in the classroom.

Embracing learner interests and passions is an outstanding way to make connections and establish relationships.

My brother and his wife, Tim and Sarah, live in Jackson Hole, Wyoming, a famous destination for skiing, mountain climbing, hiking, and whitewater rafting. My brother works on construction crews and is a photographer and my sister-in-law is a dental hygienist. They like their jobs well enough, but their passion is extreme sports: they work so that they have the money to go helicopter skiing and participate in other exhilarating outdoor activities. I'm one of only a few of their visitors who will attempt these activities with them. On my last visit they took me on an extreme hike at very high altitude as soon as I got off the plane. That's quick altitude adjustment! Engaging in extreme sports makes life worth living for my brother and sister-in-law. If the ability and opportunity to play extreme sports were taken away from them, their lives would be miserable. They are happy with the degree to which they have embraced their passions. It's why they married each other!

Someone else who truly embraces his passions, interests, and fascinations is the highly respected actor Jack Nicholson. He is a fixture at Lakers home games, has the most desirable floor seats, and often strays into the players' area of the basketball court. (Probably no one tells him to move because they remember him from *The Shining* and are scared of him!) If someone stopped him from cheering on the Lakers, his life would be miserable.

Think about your own passions, interests, and areas of fascination and how they make your life worth living. Then remember that the same is true for the students in your classroom.

While embracing student passions and interests may seem an obvious practice for teachers to undertake, the opposite is often true. When learners seem overfocused on their interests, are "obsessed" with a topic, many educators try to divert them and take the passion or interest away. In our research, Paula Kluth and I found that if an educator takes away a student's favorite interest or passion, learning is compromised, the student-teacher relationship deteriorates, and school is no longer a positive place for the learner. Teachers need to motivate all learners with the passions and fascinations that make life worth living! We can use students' interests as springboards to other topics. If we don't, we are creating potential dropouts.

> *Teachers need to motivate all learners with the passions and fascinations that make life worth living!*

Pedro: Give Him the Whale!

Pedro is a second-grader with autism whose passion is whales. One of his learning goals is to initiate and engage in communication with others. His teacher, Ms. Bardet, uses the whale topic as a springboard to get him communicating about other areas in school:

> **Ms. Bardet:** Pedro, please choose a topic you wish to talk about today.
>
> **Pedro:** I choose blue whales.
>
> **Ms. Bardet:** Okay, now look on the discussion board for the areas you need to talk about.
>
> **Pedro:** The first area is *give facts about the topic*. I need to give facts about the blue whale.
>
> The second area is *how is the topic used* in the classroom? Whales are used to help me finish my work. When I finish my work, I get a whale stamp on my paper. I like getting the whale stamp, it makes me happy! The third area is *what are other things I am doing in school*? In language arts, I'm in a literature circle. In writing, I'm working on my journal. In math, I'm learning fractions. In music, I'm playing drums.

In the past, Pedro's teaching team had deliberately avoided talking about whales, afraid that he would dwell on the topic, and Pedro had made no progress toward his learning goal of initiating and engaging in communication. Now Pedro is meeting the goal because his teachers have embraced his interest in and passion for whales and use it as a springboard to communicate about other topics and areas.

Becca: It's a Wonderful Life!

Becca is a high school learner who has been passionate about all aspects of theatre (acting, directing, stage lighting, sound effects, set design, costuming) ever since elementary school. She "lives for the stage." She begins each day—well before the starting bell—in either the main auditorium or the black box theatre and typically leaves for home after 9 p.m., getting her homework done during rehearsal breaks. Her commitment to theatre arts is exemplary. Honest and caring educators, particularly Mr. Sinclair, the school's theatre teacher/director, have given her opportunities to be an actor, a dancer, an assistant director, a stage manager, a lighting director, a sound technician, a set designer, and a costumer. She has executed each of these roles and responsibilities with competence and excels in some of them.

When she enrolled in high school Becca wanted to experience everything related to theatre. Her family encouraged her to articulate what she would like to accomplish and why. Then she made an appointment with the theatre teacher/director and shared her ideas. He listened, discussed roles she might audition for, and recommended backstage areas for her to explore. They continued their communication over the four-year period, establishing a strong, ongoing collaboration. As she gained more experience Becca became more focused and developed stronger preferences. Her theatre teacher/director honestly assessed what Becca did well and where she faced challenges. Becca's determination and self-advocacy made her theatre experiences very meaningful.

Her eyes on the prize, she has decided to study stage management in college. She feels stage management is a profession that encompasses all areas of theatre. Since she is passionate about all aspects of theatre, stage management seems the right match for her. It is also practical: stage management is one area of theatre in which people tend to be more continually employed, and can consistently practice their art. Becca is excited about applying for college, and her impressive résumé and portfolio clearly demonstrate significant background and meaningful participation in all aspects of theatre. She acknowledges Mr. Sinclair gratefully and often for helping her embrace her passions; she feels "super prepared" to study theatre in college and ultimately work in theatre professionally.

The outcome? Becca has been admitted as one of four candidates (out of over seventy applicants) in her chosen university's stage management program. It's a major feat that speaks to the benefits of Becca's impressive commitment to her passion.

> *If we understand our learners and the driving forces that motivate them—their interests, passions, and fascinations—we can promote their participation and collaboration in their education.*

FIND THE PASSION: STUDENT INTERESTS/ FAVORITES INVENTORY

I developed the Student Interests/Favorites Inventory because of my strong belief that if we understand our learners and the driving forces that motivate them—their interests, passions, and fascinations—we can promote their participation and collaboration in their education. Since today's young learners have been exposed to technology since birth, technology and multimedia are aspects of the inventory as well. It can be used with anyone and everyone.

So that all interested parties have a voice, copies of the inventory should be filled out by the student; one or more family members; and the student's prior teachers, service professionals, and para-educators. The resulting composite picture of student interests and favorite activities can be used in any and all teaching situations to improve student learning and make school a positive and meaningful place.

Interests/Favorites Inventory

Interests/Favorites Inventory for _____

Literature

_____ **Books**

Favorite Books:

_____

_____ **e-book**

_____ **Book Club**

Other:

_____

Mathematics

_____ **Math Games**

Favorite Games:

_____

_____ **Calculators**

_____ **Experiential Applications**

Other:

_____

Science

_____ **Animals/Zoology**

Favorite Animals/Areas:

_____

Pets:

_____

_____ **Biology**

_____ **Chemistry**

_____ **Physics**

Other:

_____

Social Studies/History

_____ **World History**   _____ **World Religions**

_____ **Politics**   _____ **Debate**

Other:

_____

Music

_____ **Instruments**

Favorite Instruments:

_____

Types of Music

_____ **Rock-Pop**   _____ **Country**

_____ **Soul**   _____ **Classical**

_____ **Rap-Hip Hop**   _____ **Blues**

_____ **House**   _____ **Gospel**

_____ **Jazz**   _____ **Folk**

Other:

_____

_____ **Musical Artists/Bands**

Favorite Musical Artists/Bands:

_____

_____ **Singing**   _____ **Drum Circles**

Other:

_____

Physical Activity

_____ **Fitness**   _____ **Wrestling**

_____ **Dance**   _____ **Tennis**

_____ **Baseball**   _____ **Volleyball**

_____ **Basketball**   _____ **Badminton**

_____ **Football**   _____ **Martial Arts**

Other:

_____

Art

_____ **Drawing**   _____ **Ceramics**

_____ **Painting**   _____ **Photography**

Other:

_____

(continues)

Interests/Favorites Inventory *(continued)*

Theatre & Acting

_____ **Charades**   _____ **Film/Movies**

Favorite Movies:

_____

_____ **Animation**

_____ **Magic & Entertainment Shows**

_____ **Stage Plays/Musicals**

Favorite Stage Plays/Musicals:

_____

_____ **Acting**   _____ **Sound**

_____ **Directing**

_____ **Costumes**   _____ **Costumes**

_____ **Lights**   _____ **Stage Management**

Other:

_____

Technology & Multimedia

_____ **Software & Computer Programs**

Favorite Programs:

_____

_____ **Video & Computer Games**

Favorite Games:

_____

_____ **iPod & iPad**

Other:

_____

Interpersonal Pursuits

_____ **Going Out with Friends**

Favorite Activities:

_____

Favorite Places:

_____

_____ **Telling Stories**   _____ **Telling Jokes**

Other:

_____

Architecture

_____ **Building**

Favorite Things to Build:

_____

_____ **Buildings**   _____ **Architectural Periods**

_____ **Architects**   _____ **Drawing, Drafting & Designing**

Other:

_____

Machinery

_____ **Planes**   _____ **Boats**

_____ **Trains**   _____ **Bicycles**

_____ **Autos/Race Cars**   _____ **Motorcycles & Scooters**

Other:

_____

Fashion/Beauty

_____ **Clothing**   _____ **Hair**

_____ **Accessories**   _____ **Make-up**

Other:

_____

Hobbies & Collections

Favorite Hobbies:

_____

Favorite Collections:

_____

Other:

_____

Games

_____ **Chess**   _____ **Cards**

_____ **Checkers**

Favorite Card Games:

_____

(continues)

Interests/Favorites Inventory *(continued)*

_____ **Board Games**

Favorite Board Games:

_____

Other:

_____

Culinary Arts

_____ **Cooking**

Favorite Dishes:

_____

_____ **Cooking Shows**

Favorite Shows:

_____

_____ **Restaurants**

Favorite Restaurants:

_____

Other:

_____

Helping People

_____ **Babysitting**

_____ **Charity/Charitable Causes**

Other:

_____

Stock Market

_____ **Watching the Stock Market**

_____ **Investing**

Other:

_____

Specific Professions

_____ **Teacher**

Specific Teaching Area:

_____

_____ **Professor**

Specific Teaching Area:

_____

_____ **Doctor**

Type of Doctor:

_____

_____ **Lawyer**

Type of Lawyer:

_____

_____ **Mathematician**   _____ **Scientist**

Specific Area:

_____

_____ **Business Owner**

Type of Business Owner:

_____

_____ **Artist**

Type of Artist:

_____

_____ **Writer**   _____ **Musician**

_____ **Politician**   _____ **Chef**

_____ **Business Worker**   _____ **Pilot**

_____ **Technology Specialist** _____ **Flight Attendant**

_____ **Software Designer**   _____ **Air Traffic Controller**

_____ **Video Game Designer** _____ **Driver**

_____ **Actor/Actress**   _____ **Mechanic**

_____ **Other Movie/Theatre   _____ **Fashion Designer**
      Occupations**   _____ **Beautician**

Other:

_____

How I would like to see my interests and favorites used in school:

_____

A school club I would like to join is:

_____

My dreams in life are:

_____

I would like to do this for a job someday:

_____

My recreational interests are:

_____

Example

Interests/Favorites Inventory

Interests/Favorites Inventory for Alex is a fifth-grader who enjoys computers, video games, movies, martial arts, and his dog. He is strong in math. Someday he would like to own a video game store and has done research about having a business. Alex has Asperger syndrome.

Literature

__X__ **Books**

Favorite Books: Harry Potter series, Maniac McGee, any books about computer and video games

__X__ **e-book**

__X__ **Book Club**

Other: Sticky Ninja Academy, Papa's Burgeria

Mathematics

__X__ **Math Games**

Favorite Games:

__X__ **Calculators**

__X__ **Experiential Applications**

Other: Likes working on business math concepts. Alex would love to have his own video and computer game store one day.

Science

__X__ **Animals/Zoology**

Favorite Animals/Areas:

_____

Pets: Alex enjoys his dog Jake and loves to play games with Jake such as fetch with dog toys.

_____ **Biology**

_____ **Chemistry**

_____ **Physics**

Other:

_____

Social Studies/History

__X__ **World History**   _____ **World Religions**

_____ **Politics**   __X__ **Debate**

Other: Alex has shown interest in units about inventions and innovations. He has shown leadership in debate when it has taken place in the classroom.

Music

__X__ **Instruments**

Favorite Instruments: Guitar: Alex takes interest in the guitar while playing the games Guitar Hero and Rock Band.

Types of Music

__X__ **Rock-Pop**	_____ **Country**
__X__ **Soul**	_____ **Classical**
__X__ **Rap-Hip Hop**	_____ **Blues**
__X__ **House**	_____ **Gospel**
_____ **Jazz**	_____ **Folk**

Other:

_____

__X__ **Musical Artists/Bands**

Favorite Musical Artists/Bands: ACDC, Aerosmith, LL Cool J, Beastie Boys

_____ **Singing**   _____ **Drum Circles**

Other: Alex takes martial arts classes in the community.

Physical Activity

_____ **Fitness**	_____ **Wrestling**
_____ **Dance**	_____ **Tennis**
_____ **Baseball**	_____ **Volleyball**
_____ **Basketball**	_____ **Badminton**
_____ **Football**	_____ **Martial Arts**

Other: Alex takes martial arts classes in the community.

Art

__X__ **Drawing**	_____ **Ceramics**
_____ **Painting**	_____ **Photography**

Other: Alex sketches for fun and relaxation.

(continues)

Interests/Favorites Inventory *(continued)*

Theatre & Acting

____ Charades   _X_ Film/Movies

Favorite Movies: *Loves the Phantom and Dark Knight series*

____ Animation

____ Magic & Entertainment Shows

____ Stage Plays/Musicals

Favorite Stage Plays/Musicals:

_____

____ Acting   ____ Sound

____ Directing

____ Costumes   ____ Costumes

____ Lights   ____ Stage Management

Other:

_____

Technology & Multimedia

_X_ Software & Computer Programs

Favorite Programs: *Likes any presentation software*

_X_ Video & Computer Games

Favorite Games: *Currently likes the Halo video game series*

_X_ iPod & iPad

Other:

_____

Interpersonal Pursuits

_X_ Going Out with Friends

Favorite Activities: *Gaming*

Favorite Places: *Gaming Arcades*

____ Telling Stories   ____ Telling Jokes

Other:

_____

Architecture

____ Building

Favorite Things to Build:

_____

____ Buildings   ____ Architectural Periods

____ Architects   ____ Drawing, Drafting & Designing

Other:

_____

Machinery

____ Planes   ____ Boats

____ Trains   ____ Bicycles

_X_ Autos/Race Cars   ____ Motorcycles & Scooters

Other: *Likes Audi brand cars*

Fashion/Beauty

____ Clothing   ____ Hair

____ Accessories   ____ Make-up

Other:

_____

Hobbies & Collections

Favorite Hobbies:

_____

Favorite Collections:

_____

Other:

_____

Games

____ Chess   _X_ Cards

____ Checkers

Favorite Card Games: *Enjoys Magic: The Gathering card game*

____ Board Games

Favorite Board Games:

_____

Other:

_____

(continues)

May be photocopied for classroom use. © 2013 by Patrick Schwarz from *From Possibility to Success*. Portsmouth, NH: Heinemann.

Interests/Favorites Inventory (continued)

Culinary Arts

_____ **Cooking**

Favorite Dishes:

_____

_____ **Cooking Shows**

Favorite Shows:

_____

__X__ **Restaurants**

Favorite Restaurants:

Enjoys most local pizza restaurants

Other:

_____

Helping People

_____ **Babysitting**

_____ **Charity/Charitable Causes**

Other:

_____

Stock Market

_____ **Watching the Stock Market**

_____ **Investing**

Other:

_____

Specific Professions

_____ **Teacher**

Specific Teaching Area:

_____

_____ **Professor**

Specific Teaching Area:

_____

_____ **Doctor**

Type of Doctor:

_____

_____ **Lawyer**

Type of Lawyer:

_____

_____ **Mathematician**

_____ **Scientist**

Specific Area:

_____

__X__ **Business Owner**

Type of Business Owner: Video/computer game business owner

_____ **Artist**

Type of Artist:

_____

_____ **Writer**	_____ **Musician**
_____ **Politician**	_____ **Chef**
_____ **Business Worker**	_____ **Pilot**
_____ **Technology Specialist**	_____ **Flight Attendant**
_____ **Software Designer**	_____ **Air Traffic Controller**
__X__ **Video Game Designer**	_____ **Driver**
_____ **Actor/Actress**	_____ **Mechanic**
_____ **Other Movie/Theatre Occupations**	_____ **Fashion Designer**
	_____ **Beautician**

Other:

_____

How I would like to see my interests and favorites used in school: Video games allow for free time, breaks, and rewards.

A school club I would like to join is: Debate team

My dreams in life are: To have the best and most respected local video game store where kids hang out and have gaming nights on weekends

I would like to do this for a job someday: Video/computer game store owner and game designer

My recreational interests are: Video/computer games, pizza restaurants, movies

Chapter **Three**

Think Big to Get Big

It is easy to feel hopeless in the face of statistics indicating that students with disabilities have fewer educational successes and greater quality-of-life issues than their classmates without disabilities. Yet every week I meet students, teachers, and families who transcend these statistics and are making exciting educational progress, *from disability to possibility*. This book takes this concept a step further, *from possibility to success*!

I have yet to meet a successful person who did not dream about the future and take active steps to make those dreams reality. Often these people were encouraged to dream their dreams. However, many educators draw a line in the sand regarding the dreams of students with disabilities; they suggest that these individuals are not intelligent or capable enough to achieve their dreams. Sometimes this message is so strongly communicated that the student believes he or she is not worthy to dream in the first place. This is wrong!

> **Y**et every week I meet students, teachers, and families who transcend these statistics and are making exciting educational progress, from disability to possibility.

Many people have given us great insight into their disabilities or challenges and how they used their strengths to achieve (see Grandin 2011, for example). Many of these important people had rough beginnings. (They're sometimes referred to as *late bloomers*.) The following high-achieving, highly successful people had learning challenges along the way:

- Beethoven's music teacher said, "As a composer, he is hopeless."
- Isaac Newton's work in elementary school was reported as poor.
- Einstein couldn't speak until age four; he couldn't read until age seven.
- Edison's teacher told him he was unable to learn.
- Leo Tolstoy flunked out of college.
- Louisa May Alcott was told by an editor that her writings would never appeal to the public.
- Louis Pasteur was given a rating of "mediocre" in chemistry at Royal College.
- Winston Churchill failed sixth grade.
- Henry Ford was evaluated in school as "showing no promise." (Rickets et al. 2010)